Reimagining Trauma Informed Spaces of Liberation

REIMAGINING TRAUMA INFORMED SPACES OF LIBERATION

Laura Quiros, Ph.D., LMSW

Montclair State University

Bassim Hamadeh, CEO and Publisher
Amy Smith, Associate Editorial Manager
Rachel Kahn, Production Editor
Emely Villavicencio, Senior Graphic Designer
Kylie Bartolome, Licensing Specialist
Natalie Piccotti, Director of Marketing
Kassie Graves, Senior Vice President, Editorial
Alia Bales, Director, Project Editorial and Production

Printed in the United States of America.

Contents

Introduction

It seems ironic to engage the topic of joy when we are surrounded by so much trauma. That said, it also feels imperative. Yet, social workers do not talk about joy. Joy work is not integrated into our curriculum, our supervision or into our practice. Even when we do talk about self care, joy is rarely named as a practice or emotion.

My work as a professor of social work and as a consultant has also provided me with evidence on the absence of joy in social work. I have seen students miss out on joy because they were too wedded to the group agenda or intervention and failed to notice the emotions in the room. I have witnessed white identified students focus so intently on the oppression of communities of color that they fail to notice the joy, light and beauty that said communities bring. I have seen supervisors so focused on the task element of supervision that they also miss the opportunity to name and discuss joy with their supervisees.

Noticing this gap, I decided to design workshops for social workers on the topic of joy and test my hypothesis that joy work is missing from our field. Recently, I had the opportunity to facilitate several workshops with social workers across the country on the topic of joy. I start by asking participants about joy and follow with the exploratory question "why isn't this something we promote in social work? Why don't we talk about joy?" This glaring gap in the field prompted me to write and what began as memoing and journaling turned into a book.

This book interrogates the field of social work from the places of trauma and joy. This book is my attempt to move social workers from a "presenting problem" and deficit mindset to incorporating joy into Practice without minimizing trauma. My hope is that by the end of reading this book, you will have the tools to integrate joy into your practice and that you will, personally, feel a sense of liberation for doing so.

I invited two of my international students, Huda Ahmed and Jordanne Edwards, to contribute to this book. Huda shares her narrative of being a Pakistani-Muslim woman, and how socio-political unrest, migration and displacement has shaped her ideas around home and identity, and how she learned to find joy, to heal and to flourish through her work with children.

Jordanne engages us through a case example and discussion questions, evoking you, the reader, to intentionally think deeply about how we "show up" and what emotions are present in the room, specifically in group and community work. Huda and Jordanne impacted me, and continue to do so. I have learned from their intersecting identities, their empathy, and the ways in which they negotiate their worlds. In addition, I felt it was important to look beyond a U.S. perspective to see how social work, particularly trauma and joy, shows up in other places outside of the United States. I hope you enjoy their contributions as much as I do.

I begin this book with an exploratory look and unpacking of the words "trauma" and "joy." I then move to the topic of home. This book privileges self-reflection and so within each chapter are questions for you to think about and answer independently or as a group. There is also a hope that you will move to a place of action following the reflection and processing. I encourage you to take your time, take notes in the margins or in a journal, draw, imagine, reflect, and have fun exploring different parts of yourself and social work.

One of the main objectives of this book is to help shift the deficit and monolithic mindset of social work practice to one of complexity, healing and joy. I intentionally designed this book to be small in size so that it was easy to read, carry, write-in and reference. I do not wish for this to be a textbook that sits on a shelf collecting dust, or is only read by the highly intellectual. It is student-centered and accessible while also psychologically and spiritually challenging.

CHAPTER 1

Trauma and Joy in a Person in Environment Framework

Trauma

Let's first take a look at trauma. The trauma we inherited, the trauma that surrounds us, the trauma that shows up in manifestations of being, and the trauma that can bring us growth, joy and liberation. In this book, three authors unpack, deconstruct, and position trauma as something normative that impacts the individual and collective consciousness. The authors have found, and are continuing to find, ways to integrate their traumas that allow for experiences of growth, joy and liberation to permeate. The goal is not to "overcome" the trauma; it is to acknowledge, learn from and integrate the trauma. And perhaps most important, to name and notice the manifestations of the trauma, integrating what serves us and letting go of what stops us from growth and recovery.

Can we look for the space of opportunity in that trauma, the opportunity to go deeper, the opportunity to make something beautiful out of all that has been given to us and all that has been inherited?

Joy

Next, let's introduce joy into our work. I recently facilitated a continuing education workshop for close to 200 social workers across the country, where I introduced the concept and practice of joy. Many of the participants had been in the field for years and shared that they had never explored joy with their clients. I would argue that finding joy in social work and explicitly integrating joy into our practice is essential.

First, joy is important for the mental health of social workers. The exploration of joy within the therapeutic alliance could potentially reduce the impact of vicarious traumatization.

Joy also brings positive emotion into the relationship and further expands the makers of the therapeutic alliance, making room for lightness, laughter, fun, and, ultimately, transformational healing. Imagine doing social work with a sense of rest and well-being, where you are not just responding, putting out fires, and trying to survive.

How do we, as a profession, find, occupy, and nurture joy in our practice?

Person in Environment

Throughout this book, mostly in our narratives, we define trauma in all the ways this word needs to be defined: sociopolitical, cultural, systemic, intergenerational, and individual. Which of these aspects of trauma do you tend to leave out or miss when working with clients?

We are also very much aware of the environments in which we live and the systems of oppression that further impact both the environment and the people who live in it. Environments and systems that are built on colonization and grounded in frameworks of White supremacy culture. That means that those who are traditionally marginalized by society may reexperience trauma within their environments. For example, disabled individuals do not have access to enter establishments because the establishments are not physically accessible. This inaccessibility can serve as a source of retraumatization, a reminder that the world was not physically made for their bodies. This reminder can easily manifest into internalized oppression, where the systemic oppression is internalized as an individual deficit. One benefit of acknowledging present-day, sociopolitical, and historical trauma is that it presents an opportunity for us to shift our perspective away from individual deficit framing toward the impact that history and systems have on individual well-being. Social work is a profession that is grounded in a person-in-environment framework; despite this, many social workers still solely focus on the individual, without questioning the present environments and the history of those environments in which they and our clients live. Often, social workers fail to recognize the systems of oppression that individuals are forced to navigate every day.

There may be many reasons for this sole focus on the individual and their present circumstance, without regard to history, the environment, or systems. For one, it may be because of a general disinterest in understanding environmental context, or perhaps the fear that the systems of oppression that impact the individual will be too much to handle, or, if recognized, a confrontation with ways that social workers have also been perpetuating the same types of oppression those very environments and systems were built on.

Discussion Question

1. Why else might social workers not consistently engage with the macro issues that impact micro practice? Let's spend a little time discussing this in small groups.

____

____

____

____

____

____

That said, without a sincere person in environment framework/approach, without naming and understanding the history of the many systems of oppression and exclusion communities encounter on a daily basis, we are not adhering to the professions' social justice mission. Social justice is defined by the National Association of Social Workers (2022) as "the view that everyone deserves equal economic, political and social rights and opportunities. Social workers aim to open the doors of access and opportunity for everyone, particularly those in greatest need." Opening doors of access and opportunity requires social workers to first envision what those opportunities might look like while becoming more aware of how the impact of implicit bias.

Social workers may compromise the social justice mission of social work by not helping communities envision what access and opportunity look like. This envisioning process first requires a self-reflective look at our own intersectional identities. More specifically, which aspects of our identity are oppressed and which are privileged, and in which contexts do those identities fluctuate? For example, as a woman of color working in a predominately White institution, I have often felt oppressed. I have felt oppressed by the lack of diversity in my institution, which has resulted in isolation. I have felt oppressed by stereotypes cast on me and the inequity that shows up in the implicit and explicit culture and, finally, by the invalidation of my experiences compared to my White-identified colleagues. Yet, at the same time, as a woman of color with a PhD and tenure, I am privileged and have access and opportunities that I would not have without an advanced degree and tenure.

Social workers are not situated at the same intersections of identity. While we may all identify as social workers, we differ in terms of culture, race, class, religion, ability, economic status, sexual orientation, and gender. We also differ in terms of the ways we have been socialized. Therefore, access and opportunity look different depending on one's intersections of identity. We spend time on identity, positionality, and use of self later in this book because understanding your place in the world and the lens through which you see the world is critical. Once potential areas of access and opportunities are envisioned, and bias is disrupted, we can move to the imagined feelings and experiences of joy and liberation, the cornerstone of social justice. Social justice work is grounded in liberation and joy. It is the work possibility of justice and of love.

> *"Justice is what love looks like in public."*
>
> *Cornell West*

One way to start this journey toward joy and liberation is by turning away from individual deficit and problem-focused framing. Carefully shifting the lens and case focus has the potential to lead social workers on an unknown path of joy exploration. You will read that while the authors in this book name our traumas and ways in which the authors were subjected to oppressive individuals, groups and systems, we simultaneously embrace the opportunities in those traumas while always working to confront and dismantle these systems. Here, we see very clearly the complexity in the mission of our field, working to positively disrupt systems, acknowledging the traumas, promoting healing, *and* finding opportunity in those traumas while exploring and uplifting joy and liberation. We adhere to our social work mission by envisioning what justice looks and feels like individually and collectively.

Questions to Explore While Reading This Book

1. Speaking from the "I," what is your responsibility as social workers to help our clients and consumers find joy and liberation in their worlds?

____

____

____

2. In a field that is supposed to be grounded in a strength-based ideology, social workers tend to lean on individual deficit framing, continually and consistently highlighting the struggles, challenges, and addictions of our consumers and clients. Why is this?

3. How often do we look for the space of opportunity in that trauma, the opportunity to go deeper, the opportunity to make something beautiful out of all that has been given to us and all that we have inherited?

Our hope is that you become more aware and intentional about the language and frameworks you use and the narratives you hold of yourselves and others. Additionally, begin to question the narratives you choose to share with others, including your colleagues and the clients you work with. Then, with that awareness, curiosity, and intentionality, begin to move to a place of action involving the integration of joy and liberation. During the continuing education workshop I previously mentioned, I had a participant use the term "wounded healer" to describe social workers. Using the practice of curiosity, I questioned this label out loud. I shared with the audience that, at a deeper level, language and words help construct meaning. I then asked, are we really wounded? Is there another way to identify social workers that might come from a place of strength? The group decided on "liberated healers." Before we closed the session, I shared my observation that social workers often unknowingly reinforce language and feelings of despair, marginality, and pain, and with that, in that very session, we changed our language from wounded healers to liberated healers.

Ultimately, we want to help you, the reader, explore and find the safety, joy, and liberation in working from a trauma-informed and social justice lens, thereby reimagining trauma as an opportunity for growth. This may involve creating brave spaces in the classroom, in practice, in organizations, and in our "homes" that are trauma informed, joyful, and liberated.

Discussion Question as You Begin

1. How do you define trauma? Begin with a small group discussion on the definition of trauma. Notice and name your definition of trauma. What are you defining as trauma, what and who informs this definition, and what is missing from your definition?

Let's start this reflective and tuning-in process at home, the first memory of who we were before it all began.

CHAPTER 2

Home

Michelle Obama, in her book *The Light We Carry*, talks about growing up in a physical home where safety and stability were the foundation. Where she knew what safety and stability felt like and looked like, she writes that she knows for many people, this is not the case. For example, many of the individuals and families social workers work with grew up in physical homes with addiction, economic instability, intimate partner violence, neglect, and intergenerational trauma, while others may not have had a physical place they called home.

That said, what is our responsibility as social workers to help the individuals, families, and communities we work with identify an idealized version of home? A home that feels safe and nurturing, a home that brings joy and comfort and a sense of belonging. A home where there is predictability and economic stability. Essentially, a place of residence that protects you from the outside world and when you walk through the doors you are accepted and nurtured and loved. Have we asked the individuals who seek services from us to close their eyes and imagine what "home" would look like, feel like, taste like, and smell like if it were up to them? Regardless of the places they have come from or the homes they grew up in, envisioning a new or making a corrective action to the old provides us with an opportunity for rebirth and renewal.

Yet, what most often happens is that social workers remain fixated on the problems, traumas, challenges, and struggles that are presented to them upon receiving a case. Returning to the mission of social work, as was discussed in the introduction to this book, *envisioning* a loving, safe, predictable, and nurturing home is a significant part of our social work mission. The process of envisioning allows us to momentarily escape our present reality. It takes us to a different place in our minds and is an opportunity to evoke joy in spaces that are barren and void of hope, love, and laughter. I would like to invite social workers to consider envisioning and evoking joy as a part of their practice and as a part of the social justice mission of social work.

In this chapter, we interrogate home because it is the place we first learned or did not learn about joy, and love and where patterns of behavior were formed. Social justice work is about reclaiming joy, even in environments that felt and were inherently oppressive, and for some of us that place was the homes we grew up in.

In order for social workers to envision a home of joy with the individuals, groups, and communities they work with, we must first reflect on our own experience of home. We must start with ourselves. Perhaps our home life, however that is defined, feels unexplored, taboo, or distant. Are we willing and able to revisit that, explore, and make connections to who we are today, particularly around the ways we learned about and experienced joy? Social workers ask clients to share the most intimate parts of their lives with them and yet often do not model *how* to do that. I see this reluctance to engage in self-reflection and vulnerability show up in my classroom. For example, students remain quiet around discussions on identity. My first question for students in any class I teach is, "What are the intersections of your identity?" Students do not know how to answer this question, even after I have modeled my own intersections of identity. I notice which aspects of themselves they leave out, and then we revisit this from a place of love and curiosity. I explicitly ask, "How do we engage in sincere social work practice if we are unable or sometimes unwilling to explore, for example, the intersections of our own identity and the ways we have been socialized around our identity?" Our identities that bring us some privilege, and our identities that sometimes feel marginalized and isolated. For the most part, social workers profess to remain "objective" and distanced. Traditional social work cautions against "disclosure." Yet, I wonder how we build a socially just therapeutic alliance if we are unwilling to first explore and then share parts of ourselves throughout that alliance. Remaining distant reinforces a hierarchy and is perhaps an axiomatic social work norm that further perpetuates the client deficit model.

I would like to practice the skill of use of self with you, the reader. My colleague, Dr. Karen Bagnini, and I wrote about the use of self as an anti-oppressive tool for pedagogy. Although our focus for the article was on pedagogy, many of the skills shared (Quiros & Bagnini, 2023) are applicable to practice. The use of self is a relational tool and an embodied method of teaching and practicing.

> "*We define the use of self as the intentional way social workers use our identities and our stories as a tool for anti-oppressive pedagogy, without centering the self. Defined, use of self is a relational, embodied way of teaching that involves mutuality.*" (p. 343)

In other words, through intentional self-examination, we carefully extract our own stories and use those stories to build relationships with our clients while keeping the client centered. Done with awareness and an intentional framework, sharing our stories is a powerful engagement tool that has the potential to transform a space. Storytelling is also recognized by many cultures as a healing practice. The practice skill of using oneself involves making one's positionality and intersectional identities explicit and then sharing stories about the ways one has managed struggles, challenges, and successes. This practice aids in deepening the therapeutic alliance from a social justice lens. The stories of our lived experiences enter the practice space, making us not only vulnerable but also human and fallible. Through sharing, curiosity and empathy are evoked, all of which are cornerstones of the therapeutic alliance. Like any application, timing and appropriateness are important. We share intentionally, with the goal of opening up the space for others to relate and share their own stories.

Discussion Questions

1. In your own words, what is your understanding of use of self?

____

____

____

____

____

2. How have you used this practice with your clients? If you have not, how do you imagine using it?

____

____

____

____

____

3. What about yourself, in your work with a current client, would you share? You want to begin with how you introduce yourself to your clients. What parts of your identity do you share and what parts of your identity do you withhold and why?

____

____

____

____

____

I will model use of self as I first introduce myself to you and then share with you my experience of home and my own evolution and journey back to joy.

Identity

I will begin by introducing myself to you. I identify as a Black Latina who is Jewish. I am a mother, a partner, a friend, a nurturer and an educator. I am able bodied, and my pronouns are she/her, and I wish I could add *ella* to that, but because of my father's own intergenerational trauma, he did not teach me or my brother to speak Spanish. I have struggled with identifying as both Latina and Jewish for most of my life because I felt delegitimized by society's definition of what it means and looks like to be Latina and Jewish. The single marker of identity for a Latina growing up was that you spoke Spanish, and growing up in the suburbs of New York, the single identity marker for a Jewish person was that you identified and looked White. That said, claiming my holistic identity was a journey that shifted at different times throughout my life, mostly based on context. I wonder, as I am writing, how relatable that is for some of you—the idea that our identity shifts based on context? I do believe through my research and the research of others who occupy biracial and bicultural identities, that those markers of identity have expanded and continue to expand. For example, a few of my personal markers of my Jewish identity include the value of education, the belief that I am living a purpose driven life, the practice of curiosity and inquiry, a grounding in social justice and a history that is also marked by intergenerational trauma. While a few of my personal markers of my Latina identity include my Puerto Rican and Venezuelan ancestry and ancestors, the value of family, a love and passion for life, and similarly, a grounding in social justice and a history that is marked by intergenerational trauma. I believe it is my responsibility to keep my foot on the pedal and continue to research and dialogue about the expansion of identities within the communities that I occupy. Take some time to identify your markers of identity.

Liminal Spaces

As a woman with a biracial and bicultural ancestry, I am grounded in liminality. I exist in those in-between places, "passing through a realm that has few or none of the attributes of the past or coming state (Turner, 1964). Turner (1964) terms this period a "sacred poverty in which the person has no state, property rank or kinship position." As Turner (1964) discusses, they are "no longer classified and yet not classified" (p. 48). Liminality is further defined as a prolonged state of being "betwixt and between," characterized by uncertainty and chaos (Joyce, Quiros & Waller, 2021). I now find liberation in this space because it is undefined and ripe for opportunity. I am a liminal, marginal passenger on this journey. This concept of liminality may also be applied to children of immigrants who get caught between home culture and U.S. culture.

Discussion Questions

1. What are the intersections of your identity?

2. What or who are the markers of identity for those identities?

3. How are those identities constructed?

4. Do you ever feel like you also exist in a liminal space? If so, how does it feel to be in this space?

Home

Now that I have identified myself and have spent some time reflecting on the intersections of my identity, I would like to share my experiences of home. The reason for this is that home is where we first learn about ourselves and, more specifically, about joy. My identity and the evolution of my identity are very much related to my home experience and my conceptualization of home. Home was complicated. In fact, much of the allusiveness around home was very much related to my socially constructed identity and my experiences of trauma.

After some of my own quiet reflection on what the meaning of home meant for me, I came to first realize that my mom embodied many of the attributes of home. This realization came following her passing. It was only after she passed away in 2021 that I felt a feeling of homelessness I had never felt before. I was first awakened and struck by this sense of homelessness when my now 10-year-old daughter was watching the movie *E.T.*, a 1982 American science fiction film that tells the story of Elliott, a boy who befriends an extraterrestrial, dubbed E.T., who is left behind on Earth. I walked in on the part when E.T. was trying to phone home. The extraterrestrial was stranded on Earth and was desperately trying to go back home. Out of the blue, a wave of grief took over, and I broke out in tears. Who would I call? What is home? That brief encounter with and physical reaction to the concept and placement of "home" got me thinking deeply about my recent loss and about home.

When my mom passed away in June of 2021, home became allusive. I felt a yearning sense in the pit of my stomach to go back home, but where is home, and what is home? Especially now that she was/is physically gone. If I close my eyes, I see, smell, and feel her dry hands; stale smells of cigarettes mixed with vanilla-scented candles and coffee; hordes of old photo albums populating the closets; cozy couches and fluffy pillows; warm, sweet, and savory smells of Jewish cooking, roasted chicken with orange sauce, latkes, brisket; and always vodka and Häagen-Dazs vanilla ice cream in the freezer. Our rituals were many. We would gather for the Jewish holidays; she would visit once a week and bring us our favorite items from a local café, and my girls would spend weekends and school vacations with her, and then it—and she—all disappeared, and I felt homeless.

What I did not realize was that with the grief, I was also given an opportunity to create a new and my own sense of home. Through the loss of my mother, I learned that there are emerging opportunities in grief that allow us to connect with parts and places that are elusive and undefined. I was released from the powers of attachment and caregiver-child relationships that were keeping me stuck in patterns of behavior from my childhood that remained uninterrupted. This stagnation impeded my ability to build sincere, intimate relationships, feel joy, and build a home of my own. It was as if every time I saw her, I wanted to climb onto her lap and be held—somehow trying to recreate a childhood need that was never actualized. Amid all the pain of losing my mom, I saw an opportunity for self-healing and personal growth that I could not see or feel before. The disruption to my behavior patterns freed my mind from being in the past and opened me to being in the present.

My new home was also a place filled with music, colors, and spice. Loud voices that were not angry but instead joyful. A place where we could talk about anything, where ancestors were honored, and traditions were passed on. Home was the beach, the salty air, and the sound of waves. While I did not find these attributes in my childhood home, I did find them in trips to Puerto Rico as a child, and I was able to integrate these sights, smells, tastes, and sounds into my new home. How many of us have been somewhere, and that place just feels like home?

While intergenerational trauma often cuts us off from cultural experiences that have the potential to nurture us, we do have the agency to rediscover, recreate, and integrate our ancestry in ways never imagined. For example, the discrimination that my father and his family experienced blocked the integration of our Latine ancestry, and through my own exploration and healing, I have rediscovered the beauty of my culture and the ancestral gifts that have been passed on. I acknowledge the pain of discrimination and what was lost while also embracing the beauty of what is and what I can claim as my own.

My current home, physically, psychologically, and spiritually, is built on the foundation of safety, belonging, and joy. I have never appreciated joy and safety as much as I do now. In fact, when friends check in and ask me how I am, my response is, "My home is warm and safe and stable. We eat dinner together as much as we can; my kids sleep through the night, and unless it is externally imposed, no one is dangerously anxious." My children know that they are safe at home. My children are also biracial and bicultural, and they are grounded in the complexity of their identities. We talk about what that means and the differences and similarities between us: how my oldest passes for White, identifies as biracial, Latina, and Jewish, and my youngest identifies as Black, Jewish, and Caribbean, strangers continually question how they are related. One of my primary responsibilities as their mother is to build a home where we can talk and question and love from our deepest parts, where home is our respite, the safe foundation that we all return to at the end of each day. Through our open communication and affection, I am inoculating them against the potential damage and microaggressions they may face from the outside world. I share that we are all whole, not half of anything, but whole, made up of many different, diverse, and beautiful parts.

For many, safety is a privilege; that said, can we help our clients envision what safety looks like, feels like, and smells like?

Discussion Questions

1. How has your definition of home changed over time? Home is a construct that seems fixed for many, but in reality, it is flexible.

____

____

____

____

____

____

2. Where is home for you?

____

____

3. What does home look like, feel like, smell like?

4. How do the intersections of your identity impact home for you?

References

Joyce, P. A., Quiros, L., & Waller, B. (2021). Honoring liminality: teaching critical and race-gendered approaches in doctoral social work education. *Social Work Education, 41*(5), 993–1005.

Obama, M. (2022). *The light we carry.* Random House.

Quiros, L. & Bagnini, K. (2023). Use of self as an anti-oppressive tool for pedagogy. *Journal of Teaching in Social Work*, *43*(3), 342–352.

Turner, V. (1969). *The ritual process: Structure and anti-structure.* Cornell.

CHAPTER 3

Joy

Now that we have situated ourselves at home, let's explore our earliest memories of joy. Joy literally means the feeling of pleasure, while liberation is the release and freedom from struggle and from oppression.

I recently asked my MSW students what joy means to them. Their responses varied. Some named peace of mind and being able to be present, while others named physical locations such as the beach and their bedrooms. Students named the act of building community and solidarity as joy. They tapped into smells, sounds, and colors, such as the smell of their mom's cooking, the sounds of waves, the color purple, laughter, and the act of playing and being with their children. One student asked me, can you tell me what joy is and what I should do to access it in my practice? This question made me pause. Joy is not an intervention. I told the student that my definition of joy and how I find joy is most likely very different from theirs. The work lies in being able to access and define joy first for yourself and then, from a place of love and curiosity, with your clients. I often worry that social work students lean too heavily on interventions found in handouts and textbooks rather than what they have access to internally. Are social work educators, including supervisors, making space in classrooms and in supervision for students and practitioners to access what they have inherited and what lives inside?

Yet, if joy is essential for social work practice, both for the practitioner and for the client, why is it left out? Why is the movement toward joy, perhaps, a radical shift in our social work practice? Let's keep this question front and center as we move through this chapter. First, let's begin with ourselves. Take some time in small groups to locate yourself in joy.

Discussion Questions

1. What is your earliest memory of joy within your home?

2. Was it a constant and consistent state of being, or was it sporadic, inconsistent, and contextual?

3. What does joy look like and feel like for you?

____

____

____

____

____

4. What parts of our early home life are we carrying with us, clinging to, passing on and letting go of, as it relates to joy?

____

____

____

____

____

Use of Self: Relocating My Joy

I have a vivid picture in my mind of my 5-year-old self. In this picture, I am at my nana's house. My hair was in two pigtails, my smile wide with a missing front tooth. I had on a white three-quarter sleeve T-shirt with a rainbow in the middle. This little girl was happy, carefree, silly, and joyful. She liked to play dress up, swim, and take naps.

And then, at age 6, the world as she knew it changed before her eyes. I experienced my first adverse childhood experience: the death of my 4-month-old brother named Daniel. That childhood trauma at the age of 6 clouded my earliest memory of joy as new and self-protective parts emerged (Schwartz, 2021). Life, as I knew and imagined it to be, shifted.

I was 6 years old, and it was Christmas Eve. My memory tells me that I was home, my aunt was babysitting me, my dad was at work finishing up a half day at the office, and my mom was running last-minute errands. Daniel, my 4-month-old baby brother, was asleep in his crib. It was snowing, and it was sure to be a white Christmas. My aunt stepped out to go to the store, and so for just a brief time, I was home alone. Daniel was my everything, and as a good big sister, I made sure to check on him regularly, especially the day before Christmas. The house was quiet, and I snuck into his room, careful not to wake him. I remember looking into his crib; the memory remains very vivid; something felt off. He seemed to be sleeping, a little too soundly, on his stomach. At that moment, the phone rang. I left his room and picked up the phone to hear my dad asking me how I was and that he was on his way home. My memory tells me I said, "Daddy, something is wrong with Daniel." To that, he answered, "I am sure he is fine. I will be home soon." We hung up, and within minutes, my mom returned; the details remain blurry, but what I do remember is my mom running down the stairs with Daniel in her arms, yelling, "My baby isn't breathing." Something WAS wrong with Daniel. That was it; we made our way to the hospital, escorted halfway by the police, and within minutes after arriving, a police officer found me in the waiting room. He brought me a cup of juice and cookies from the vending machine and delivered the news that Daniel was gone. Daniel died in his sleep from sudden infant death syndrome on Christmas Eve.

If only I had checked on him earlier. That was the thought that was stuck in my head for years after that childhood trauma occurred. The day before, I remember holding Daniel in his rocking chair, saying out loud, "What would I do if anything ever happened to you?" Magical thinking for a 6-year-old is very common, and so I went through the steps before and after I went into Daniel's room many, many times. The "if onlys" became obsessive. I swore I would never verbalize out loud how much I cared for another person for fear that something bad might happen. And I really truly believed that I was responsible for Daniel's death. The joy of that little girl began to fade, and other parts began to emerge. That little girl smiling with her rainbow shirt on, who loved to swim and play and laugh, was visited by fear, anxiety, hypervigilance, and sorrow, and the image of Daniel in his crib would not go away.

At 6, joy became something fleeting, experienced in moments but never stable. It was an emotion and a feeling I grew to be scared of. Too much joy meant something bad was soon to follow.

It was not until very recently in my own therapy that I could access her, that little 6-year-old girl, by engaging in deep work with my therapist using an integrated family systems model (Schwartz, 2021). That little girl's memory was clouded by the experience of losing Daniel, and those post-trauma reactions still inhabited my present life. What I came to realize was that while this story of what happened to her is very sad, those qualities inherent in that joyful child had the potential to reemerge. Joy has started to reemerge in my home and in my life in ways I did not know were possible.

Reflecting on our work with consumers, clients, families, groups, and communities, do we ask questions about joy? Do we help people explore the many parts of themselves pre- and post-trauma? Or do we remain fixated on the oppressions, challenges, and struggles?

Discussion Questions

1. What resonates for you in this story? Why does it resonate?

___

___

2. What do you understand about "magical thinking" in social work practice? What other mechanisms are at play or are seen in response to childhood trauma? Can you give examples from your life or from your practice?

I'd like for us to revisit the question that was presented early in this text: What are the axiomatic norms in social work that perhaps need to be reconsidered to enable radical shifts to joy and liberation?

In this next chapter, we meet our second author, a Muslim woman from Pakistan who is in her thirties. It was intentional not to have this book be U.S. centric but rather to capture the stories of two of my students who are born and lived outside of the United States. Both women have lived and studied experiences of trauma, joy, and liberation. We read about the trauma of colonization and the impact of that trauma on collective consciousness, identity, and interpersonal relationships. We read about alternate meanings of "home" and the author's personal understanding of trauma, healing, resilience, and liberation. I hope you find Huda's story as impactful as I do.

Reference

Schwartz, R. (2021). *No bad parts: Healing trauma and restoring wholeness with the internal family systems model.* Sounds True, Incorporated.

CHAPTER 4

Home and Identity Through the Lens of a Pakistani Muslim Woman

By Huda Ahmed

Following suit of the previous chapters, I will also begin by situating myself in this world. I am a Muslim woman from Pakistan in my 30s. Most facets of my identity are out of my control. They are not only how the world sees me but the lens through which I see the world.

I am a teacher at heart and a social worker by profession. These parts of my identity are what I choose every day, and to do right by the profession, I must be aware of how the cultural and religious nuances shape the experiences of individuals and communities I work with. To do that, I must first reflect on the unique challenges and strengths that arise from my own intersecting identities. By embracing my identity and using it as a source of strength, I can provide a more holistic and empathetic approach to my practice.

Being a social worker from Pakistan, I carry the weight of my country's history, its struggles, and its resilience. I recognize the impact of colonization, sociopolitical challenges, and intergenerational trauma on the individuals and communities I serve. I consider it my responsibility to engage in continuous learning, unlearning, and self-reflection to address biases, challenge oppressive systems, and advocate for justice and empowerment.

Through this chapter, I aim to shed light on trauma-informed social work practice through my unique lens. I will also talk about my home, the trauma I inherited from my ancestors, and the effects of colonization, which shake the foundations of my region even today. I will talk about how I see trauma influencing our mind, body, and soul. And then, with reference to my experience working with children, I will talk about resilience and meaning-making beyond our pains.

I believe that by exploring the crossroads of cultural identity, faith, and the layers of intergenerational, sociopolitical, and interpersonal trauma we have gone through as a people, we can better understand the intricacies that inform the lives of those seeking support and healing.

> *"Trauma in a person, decontextualized over time, looks like personality.*
>
> *Trauma in a family, decontextualized over time, looks like family traits.*
>
> *Trauma in a people, decontextualized over time, looks like culture."*
>
> *Resmaa Menakem, "My Grandmother's Hands"*

Discussion Question

1. Reflecting on this quote, what comes up for you? Can you share specific examples with one another in a way that personalizes this quote?

____

____

____

Colonization: My Ancestors Losing Their Homes and Identities

As a South Asian individual with a lineage deeply intertwined with the trauma of colonization, I carry within me the stories of my ancestors who were uprooted from their ancestral lands, seeking refuge and a sense of belonging.

When I think of home, I think of the slightly chilly evening of the fall of 2022 as I sat at the dining table at my sister's house in Austin, Texas, with my father's older cousin, Raffat Anwar, as we devoured a bowl of Nihari with some freshly baked naan. He tells us how the meal reminds him of his ancestral village in Bazidpur, in the Samastipur district of Bihar, India, a place he remembers as if it was yesterday. He talks about that place often, as if it were etched in his memory, forever resonating with a sense of nostalgia and longing.

In another memory, I find myself lying next to my grandmother in Islamabad, Pakistan, her aged hands tightly clasping mine. She shares stories of her childhood, a trip to Kashmir with her father, and the family home in Hyderabad Deccan prior to the Partition of the Indian subcontinent. It was a time of great upheaval as my grandmother's family, like countless others, was forced to abandon their cherished abode and embark on a perilous journey toward an uncertain future. Among the narratives that shape my family's history is that of my grandmother's sister, Shahida Gilani. Whenever she visited, she would recount the harrowing night of 1947 when her family hastily packed their belongings and left their home forever. Under the cover of darkness, they sought safety, boarding an airplane carrying weapons and arms.

The journey of my paternal and maternal families mirrors the larger tale of partition and migration. They traversed from Bazidpur to Hyderabad, from Patna to Dhaka, and ultimately settled in Karachi, Pakistan. Their movements were not born out of choice but driven by the relentless waves of violence and displacement that accompanied the Partition. The trauma of those times, marked by unimaginable atrocities and loss of life, reverberates through the collective consciousness of the South Asian subcontinent. The Partition of 1947 and the subsequent division in 1971 with the birth of Bangladesh scarred the region.

Every person in the South Asian subcontinent holds a partition story. These stories are marked by harrowing escapes, heartbreaking separations from loved ones, and acts of compassion as strangers opened their hearts and homes to those seeking safety. Everyone has a story of how the world changed in front of their very eyes. Yet, as a society, we often fail to confront and openly discuss the trauma we have endured.

Discussion Question

1. What is your story?

My ancestors were fortunate to have survived those turbulent times. The women were protected. The children and elders alive. But they had to start over with absolutely nothing, and as the years of their lives withered away, and as the pressure of providing and surviving was alleviated, the pain of loss of their identity, their sense of belonging, their home, spoke louder than any other story they told us. My grandparents, forever, carried those parts of themselves in their hearts as they moved on to rebuild their lives, anchoring on nothing but faith and hope for a future where their struggles seemed worth it.

The colonizers supposedly left the region in 1947, but the deep, insidious effects of their rule still remain, which instilled a sense of inferiority, intolerance toward diversity, and erasure of the region's rich culture, history, and languages.

The trauma of colonization extends beyond the historical period and continues to shape contemporary Pakistani society. It has influenced the collective consciousness, contributing to a deep sense of post-colonial hangover of identity crisis and a constant struggle for self-determination. Even society's perception of beauty for women remains centered around being "gori" (fair-skinned), perpetuating a harmful standard influenced by White supremacist ideals, capitalism, and internalized racism, as illustrated by the popularity of skin-lightening creams in advertisements. The legacy of colonization has created a complex relationship with Western ideals and cultural influences, with ongoing debates about the balance between the preservation of cultural heritage and the adoption of modernity. Amid this polarization and changing world, I find an increasing number of South Asians struggling to define and reclaim their identities. Where do we belong in this world?

Recognizing and addressing the trauma of colonization is crucial for understanding the challenges and aspirations of society. It requires acknowledging the lingering effects of historical injustices, fostering cultural pride and resilience, and advocating for equitable systems that promote healing, empowerment, and decolonization.

Discussion Questions

1. Have you thought about the trauma of colonization before? What comes up for you as you are reading this story?

____

____

____

____

____

____

Fragmented Roots: Belonging in the Diaspora

When I think of home, I think of gathering around the dining table at my grandfather's house in Karachi and laughing with my cousins. I remember the adults talking about political unrest in the country and where they should go next. Slowly, one by one, each family at a time, my uncles and aunts moved out of the country to find new homes. As we grew older, got educated, and moved on with our lives, most of us traveled far and wide, and settled in different parts of the world. But we carried those parts of us within our bodies, without ever knowing it – the quirky head nod, the food, the traditions, the songs – that were stripped away from our ancestors. *It is in our blood, in our bodies. It is not just the genes and the language or culture that we carry.* It is also the pain, the loss, and the suffering. Where is home when all your life, all you've ever known is the desire to flee? We see present-day examples of this in Europe, Southern America, and the atrocities happening in Ukraine, including war crimes of "rehoming" children.

Sadly, that is what the culture of the educated classes of countries like Pakistan and India has become—to find an opportunity somewhere in the world and leave the Global South as soon as you can. It is only when we stop running that we realize the magnitude of how much we have left behind and how much of that loss we still carry in our bodies. It is not just a "brain drain" for a region when all the educated, well-meaning young people leave to find a better life for themselves—it is also a draining of hearts. It is emotionally taxing to leave a place you once called home because it no longer gives you a sense of security or stability. It is a loss not just for the country but even for the people who leave to migrate to a new land, not knowing where they truly belong.

Discussion Questions

1. Have you ever had to leave a place you once called home?

____

____

____

____

____

____

2. Have you worked with clients who have had to leave a place they call home?

____

____

____

____

____

____

This profound sense of loss, stemming from sociopolitical and intergenerational trauma, often manifests as interpersonal trauma, infiltrating our intimate relationships. Not knowing who we truly are or where we genuinely belong, we find ourselves compelled to conform, contorting our body language, accents, and demeanor to survive in foreign cultures where we hope to establish new roots. This constant shape-shifting to fit the mold of expectations leaves us feeling adrift, homeless, and detached from any grounding sense of self.

In this search for belonging, we grapple with the yearning to rediscover our true essence and reclaim the parts of ourselves that have been scattered across time and space. It is an ongoing journey of self-discovery, healing, and reconnection—an endeavor to reconcile the ruptures caused by displacement and to forge a renewed sense of identity and purpose. As we navigate this complex landscape of identity and belonging, we must strive to cultivate compassion, understanding, and empathy—for ourselves and for others who share similar journeys. It is through acknowledging our shared experiences of longing and loss that we can begin to heal the wounds of the past and nurture a sense of home within ourselves, wherever we may find ourselves in the world.

Nurturing Resilience: Transforming Lives Through Trauma-Informed Care and Education

During my quest for a place to call home and a sense of purpose, I dedicated 3 years to working in a remarkable trauma-informed, mother-child education system in Karachi, Pakistan, known as the Kiran Foundation. Situated in the heart of Lyari, a neighborhood often misunderstood as violent and unsafe, this organization operated within the reality of a community scarred by immense pain and turmoil. Despite their hardships, the residents of Lyari displayed unimaginable resilience and joy. The children and youth, particularly affected by a war that had nothing to do with them, experienced significant loss as they were pushed to the sidelines—ignored, neglected, and often abused. My transformative experience of working with children in this trauma-informed space reshaped not only their lives but also my own. It opened my eyes to recognize behavioral patterns that offered insights into the human experience of trauma and healing. I discovered that what we receive in our formative years influences what we give back to the world unless we actively break free from the cycle of intergenerational trauma.

In childhood, our vulnerable selves are highly receptive, absorbing the environment around us like a sponge. If we are enveloped in love and stability, those qualities become part of us. Conversely, if toxicity and unpredictability surround us, those elements seep into our being. Our early experiences shape our inner scripts, which we unconsciously repeat to ourselves and which are reflected in our interactions as we grow older.

We often perpetuate what we have internalized from childhood; hence, individuals who have endured abuse may perpetrate abuse themselves. After years of trauma, violence, and poverty, it is no surprise that children develop aggression and intolerance toward themselves or others, perpetuating the "Cycle of Abuse." Individuals raised in stressful environments often become hypervigilant, constantly in fight, flight, or freeze mode. Like a porcupine driven by fear, they navigate the world with their defenses up, conveying the message, "I will hurt you before you hurt me." These individuals are frequently seen as aggressive or overly reactive when, in reality, they are responding based on their early survival instincts and the environment they grew up in.

To break the cycle of abuse, individuals require a safe space (which may or may not be home) and the presence of at least one caring adult in their lives who helps to ground them, initiating their healing process.

Equipped with tools that foster self-awareness and empathy, individuals can learn to regulate their thoughts and emotions, adopting healthier coping mechanisms. This empowers them to transcend their traumas, dismantle toxic patterns and scripts, and ultimately lead a life of purpose and significance.

Through a trauma-informed lens, we look beyond individuals' presenting behaviors, which may manifest as aggression or withdrawal, and strive to create nurturing environments where they feel safe and supported and can embark on their healing journey. As care providers, it is our collective responsibility to cultivate empathy and support. We must believe that all behavior is a means of seeking connection, and with the right support, individuals can transform their lives, not just healing but flourishing. Liberation from pain and suffering becomes possible as they embark on a journey of finding meaning and purpose.

Please spend some time reflecting on these last few paragraphs. Take out a pen and piece of paper and/or write in the margins. What comes up for you?

As social workers, educators, health-care providers, legal aid providers, legislators, and policymakers, it is imperative that we embrace this trauma-informed lens when making decisions. By doing so, we can create a conducive environment that supports individuals in their pursuit of self-connection and healthy relationships with others.

Trauma-Informed Case Study: Kiran Foundation

At the Kiran Foundation, we transcended the boundaries of conventional education, incorporating elements that facilitated the development of a profound self-awareness and understanding of others for both children and adults. By enabling individuals to regulate their thoughts and emotions, we aimed to equip them with the tools necessary to navigate life's challenges. What made this educational approach unique was its commitment to engaging parents and caregivers in the learning process, addressing generational inequities, systemic disparities, and social injustices. Systems approach. We acknowledged our shared humanity—the fact that we are all imperfect, adaptable, and constantly evolving emotional beings. We recognized that life is far from easy, but within each of us lies the potential to cultivate joy, strength, and resilience. Together, we embarked on an ongoing journey of curious exploration, delving into the depths of our inner and outer worlds. Learning from one another, we grew and evolved as a community of visionary thinkers and world shifters.

Through a wide range of creative modalities such as art, play, music, sports, dance, meditation, yoga, Qi Gong, and more, we came together every day, fostering a sense of belonging and purpose. Together, we forged a community that challenged the status quo, embracing the power of education to empower individuals, families, and the entire community. By instilling resilience and fostering holistic well-being, we aimed to transform lives and build a brighter future for all.

In our pursuit of building resilient communities, we celebrated the beauty of our shared humanity and the limitless potential within each individual. By offering trauma-informed education, we worked hand in hand with the people of Lyari, nurturing their strengths and supporting them on their transformative journeys toward healing and growth.

This process of change would not have been possible if we had not taken the time to deeply understand and address the root causes of their traumas. As I reflect on our collective efforts, I am reminded of a powerful quote from John C. Maxwell's book, *Failing Forward: How to Make the Most of Your Mistakes*, which resonates deeply with our mission of instigating change:

> *"People change for four different reasons. People change when they are hurt enough, they have to; when they see enough, they're inspired to; when they learn enough, they want to, and when they receive enough, they are able to."*

Discussion Questions

1. Have you ever felt uprooted or lost your sense of home and identity? If yes, was it enforced or by choice? How has the sociopolitical climate of your region shaped your sense of home and identity?

____

____

____

____

____

____

2. Have you ever had to shape-shift or change your name, accent/body language to better "fit in"? How does that feel? How can we make our practice inclusive so that people do not have to change themselves in order to feel like they belong?

3. How can we break the cycle of abuse or trauma in our lives and allow ourselves to change and grow in areas where we currently feel inhibited?

CHAPTER 5

Liberation and Joy

Liberated spaces are not restricted or psychologically regulated. These spaces are colorful and feel warm, open, and accessible. Liberated spaces feel free of judgment even on the worst of days. These spaces feel brave, silly, curious, nonbinary, nuanced, complex, communal, and collaborative. These spaces are grounded in dialogue, not debate; processing is welcome, no matter how long it takes. Liberated spaces are spaces of freedom where we can move, breathe, and be. Are the spaces that we occupy as social workers liberated spaces that are intentionally designed to encourage joy? For a profession that often emphasizes strengths, it is ironic that joy does not always translate into the spaces we cultivate.

I purport that the call for more joy is not a superficial endeavor but a radical practice of unpacking what is already there. We already have the tools to do this work. From being trained in anti-oppressive approaches, we understand how power dynamics inform the environments of our client's habitat.

Joy is a legitimate pathway to tapping into the complexity of the effects present in the trauma-informed spaces we work in. Focusing solely on the deprivation caused by trauma and other atrocities can lead to a stagnation of *un-living.* The third author, Jordanne Edwards, identifies as a Black Jamaican woman who grew up mostly in Kingston, Jamaica, where she learned to take great pride in Afro-centric identity, culture, and resistance. This Caribbean-informed sense of resilience to live and thrive continues to inspire her social work practice and research with various communities around the world, including asylum seekers, Indigenous peoples, and anti-racism activists. As Jordanne shares, "*Joy* is a disruptive and legitimate emotion that is not only present but possible in community-based social work." Next, Jordanne shares an illustration of joy with us from her social work practice in Jamaica.

Joy Is Already in the Room

By Jordanne Edwards

This example comes from my social work practice in Jamaica, where I worked with and for several human rights-based organizations. Within this role, I was once invited to facilitate a session at a youth club. It was meant to be a "capacity building" and rights awareness event. I had planned to facilitate group exercises that fostered conversations around gender equality because gender-based violence/ violence against women was a topical issue and experience within that community. However, an urgent work matter came up at the office which needed to be addressed. Staying back meant that I was going to be almost an hour late. Fortunately, a youth advocate from the community was able to substitute until my arrival.

Rushing into the room, I was prepared to mediate what I assumed would be heavy, maybe even heated conversations. Instead, I was greeted by the sounds of drums beating, hands clapping and feet stomping melodiously in unison. A vivacious member of the group was in the midst of making a witty joke as I approached the front row with flyers and human rights stickers almost sliding out of my hand. The room erupted in laughter and dance. It became clear that there was no sense in disrupting the flow of the meeting with my agenda. The main topic was addressed but through body movement. People didn't just want to talk, they wanted to flow and release. Their idea of making a space to talk about violence was to counter it with freedom of expression—to loosen the body. "Awareness-building" was centered in the body, grounded in cultural and ancestral expression not of resistance, but relinquishing and leaning into joy.

Joy was not on the agenda, it emerged naturally. People felt safe enough not just to show daunting emotions but to show the wittier side of their character. I'm not sure my planned facilitation would have evoked a similar reaction. My professional training and workshop template, dictated a deep dive into the despair of violence and how to *overcome.* I was unintentionally closed off to the other possibilities present in the room. I imagine that similar to other sessions, had I started the meeting, my focus on patriarchy and gender inequalities would have beckoned to the language and emotion common to human rights infractions such as disappointment, anger and frustration. While these are all valid, it is interesting to reflect on how it innocuously obscures the joy that is already in the room. Creativity and artistic expression isn't new to liberatory community practice and the benefits are well documented in critical research (Boal, 2000; Ottemiller & Awais, 2016). I expected to walk into a room, offering activities that would help to inspire without considering that they were already inspired. *In creating literal agendas with action points, are we reflecting on how our professional practices inform how a community thinks and feels their way through collective issues?*

I'd often struggle to document these experiences under achieving the corporate KPIs set out to measure the programme's efficacy. Instead we relied on the statistics of the number of communities we engaged with on the ground and online. Pictures of laughter and dance were mainly shared as a representation of the positive impact our programs were having on the community. As opposed to speaking more deeply about what they actually represented. My immediate team and I played two roles: one for the managerial stakeholders and one for the community. The real work was being in the community and diving into the emergent linguistics and affect they revealed. For instance, the youth group created their own online group to share funny memes that would help each other to start the day. That too was community work unfolding. This story illustrates how joy and ways of being can serve to disrupt the normative practices of social work. *How can social workers be better prepared to engage with pleasure and joy?*

My recommendation here is for social workers to do a mapping exercise of how we occupy spaces. Before entering or inviting communities into a space ask questions such as: *Is my agenda allowing space for a dynamic range of expression? How can I create space for a complex range of language and emotions that may want to be recognized in community? How can I better reflect a community's embodiment practices in the services that I offer? Is my organization of practice prepared to implement changes that better align with the community?*

***

Jordanne invites us to intentionally think about, collectively discuss and move into action around joy in micro, mezzo and macro practice. First consider the times joy has shown up in practice. Next, she invites us to pay attention to emotions in the room. For so long, our field has encouraged us to void our emotions, yet emotions are critical to human connection. The final discussion questions ground us in community work and emotional safety.

Discussion Questions

1. If joy shows up in your practice, notice it. Please share some examples with one another. Commit to an activity that will center joy in your practice.

____

____

____

2. During group activities, I invite you to reflect on and discuss this question: What are the emotions in the room telling me about the community's/individual's experiences? *What do communities tell us about their living?* Think specially about trauma and joy and the emotions connected to these words. What is felt in the room?

3. While imagining and planning community work, think about how you can create emotional safety for community members to openly express themselves and step into their joy. Please be concrete and move into action.

____

____

References

Boal, A. (2000). *Theater of the oppressed*. Pluto Press.

Ottemiller, D. D., & Awais, Y. J. (2016). A model for art therapists in community-based practice. *Art Therapy*, *33*(3), 144–150.

Conclusion

Social Workers; Restorers of the Soul

I often call social workers restorers of the soul, those who help us, as a collective, revisit and restore our souls from before the trauma, not to minimize or erase the trauma but to unearth and evoke those parts that were both injured and covered by the manifestations of trauma by the coping mechanisms. I was asked in a recent training by a participant who shared that they identified as an atheist, what I meant by soul. After some thought I shared that I define soul as that part inside of me, my essence, the part that has not been touched by my traumas.

Given all that you have read thus far, I would like you to spend this final chapter grounding yourself in your identity as a social worker. I had the opportunity to go on a soul journey in 2022. Lying on a bed, listening to chimes, I was guided to find that place of reconnection with my soul. My journey landed me on a beach and eventually in the water. As someone who has always had a connection to the ocean, perhaps because of my ancestry, I found peace submerged underwater, mermaid-like—gliding with schools of fish around me. In my journey, at different moments, I was met by women who were bejeweled and in community with me. I was surrounded by my women friends, mentors, and ancestors—it was warm and peaceful and clear and simply beautiful. My movements were fluid and strong, and I took risks to travel further and deeper into the ocean until it was time to return.

Discussion Questions

1. What would be the place you return to for healing?

____

____

____

____

____

____

2. As you reflect on your social work journey, what has been missing from your practice?

____

____

____

____

____

____

3. In a world filled with so much trauma, can we still incorporate joy into our work? Our clients are not inherently oppressed; they are oppressed by the systems they live in, and while it is our responsibility to help dismantle those systems, it is also our responsibility to help our clients reclaim their joy and help create liberated spaces.

____

____

____

____

____

I see this book as a gift for you to live and practice in spaces of joy. My hope is that you find ways to integrate trauma, finding opportunities for growth and for renewal. Make joy an everyday practice in your life.

I would not be in the place that I am today without my community. I am writing this book on the heels of turning 50 where I spent a week on Martha's Vineyard surrounded by my loved ones, those who uplift me, help ground me, dance and laugh with me. I am so grateful.

Thank you to my community. Thank you, Huda and Jordanne, for your heartfelt contributions and thank you Kassie Graves for your support and access. This text is dedicated to my girls Carla and Izzy and to my partner Lloyd who has helped me recreate a home of safety, laughter, love and joy.

My love for the field of social work is very real. I just want us to do better by living sincerely by our mission which includes a person- in-environment framework, a strength-based ideology, empathic accountable, justice, love and always in service.

Index

www.ingramcontent.com/pod-product-compliance
Ingram Content Group UK Ltd.
Pitfield, Milton Keynes, MK11 3LW, UK
UKHW021829270726
14058UKWH00001B/51

9 798823 313346